D0822226

Birds of Prey

Written and Illustrated
by Todd Telander

FALCONGUIDES

GUILFORD, CONNECTICUT
HELENA, MONTANA

AN IMPRINT OF ROWMAN & LITTLEFIELD

To my wife, Kirsten, my children, Miles and Oliver, and my parents, all of whom have supported and encouraged me through the years.

FALCONGUIDES®

An imprint of Rowman & Littlefield
Falcon, FalconGuides, and Outfit Your Mind are registered trademarks of Rowman & Littlefield.

Distributed by NATIONAL BOOK NETWORK

British Library Cataloguing-in-Publication Information available

Library of Congress Cataloging-in-Publication Data

Telander, Todd.
  Birds of prey / by Todd Telander.
    pages cm. — (Falcon pocket guide)
  Includes bibliographical references and index.
  ISBN 978-1-4930-0223-8
  1. Birds of prey. I. Title.
  QL677.78.T45 2014
  598.9—dc23
                                2014035108

∞™ The paper used in this publication meets the minimum requirements of American National Standard for Information Sciences—Permanence of Paper for Printed Library Materials, ANSI/NISO Z39.48-1992.

Contents

Introduction

Birds of prey, commonly known as raptors, are typically defined as those birds that feed on other vertebrate animals. They also possess sharp, hooked bills and strong talons that they use together to tear apart the flesh of their prey. This group includes the diurnal raptors (meaning they are most active during the day), including the vultures, eagles, hawks, kites, harriers, falcons, and osprey, as well as those that are active mainly at night—the owls. And although not technically birds of prey, I have included also the shrikes, which are raptorial in their habits despite being classified with the passerines. Birds of prey are found in nearly every habitat across the continent, from the Arctic Circle to the Mexican border, and even in the most populated urban centers. This guide is an introduction to fifty-five birds of prey that occur regularly in North America, from the massive California Condor, saved from the brink of extinction, to the majestic Bald Eagle, to the tiny Elf Owl of southwestern deserts. May you enjoy your exploration into this fascinating group of birds!

Notes About the Species Accounts

Order

The order of species listed in this guide is based on the latest version of the *Checklist of North American Birds,* published by the American Ornithologists' Union.

Names

For each entry I have included the bird's common name as well as the scientific name. Since common names tend to vary regionally, or there may be more than one common name for each species, the universally accepted scientific name of genus and species (such as *Buteo lagopus* for the Rough-legged Hawk) is a more reliable identifier. Also, you can often learn interesting facts about a bird from the English translation of its Latin name. For instance, the term *buteo* is Latin for a kind of hawk, and *lagopus* is Latin meaning "rabbit foot," referring to the feathered legs of this bird.

Families

Birds of prey, like all birds, are grouped into families based on similar traits, behaviors, and genetics. When trying to identify an unfamiliar bird, it is often helpful to first place it into a family, which will limit your search to a smaller group. For example, if you see a raptor in open country during the day with narrow, pointed wings and fast, direct flight, you can begin your search in the family group of Falconidae (falcons), and narrow your search from there. Conversely, a large bird soaring high in the air on broad wings is most likely of the group of hawks (Accipitridae).

Size

The size listed for each bird is the average length from the tip of its bill to the end of its tail, if the bird was laid out flat. Sometimes females and males vary in size, and this is mentioned in the text (among the birds of prey, females are often larger than males). Size can be misleading if you are looking at a small bird that happens to have a very long tail or bill. It may be more effective to use the bird's relative size, or judge the size difference between two or more species.

Range

Range refers to the geographical distribution of a species. Some birds of prey, such as the Red-tailed Hawk and the Great Horned Owl, can be found in suitable habits across North America, while others have extremely limited ranges, such as the Aplomado Falcon, which is found only in a small area of southeastern Texas. Examples of ranges are regions such as the Southwest, eastern United States, Rocky Mountains, Pacific Northwest, and so on. Also consider that vagrant birds are capable of showing up in areas well outside of their normal range, while some birds may be absent from where they "should" occur.

Habitat

A bird's habitat is one of the first clues to its identification. This describes the ecosystem type within a range, such as woodlands, grasslands, tundra, desert, mountains, riparian areas, or urban areas. Note the environment where you see a bird and compare it to the description listed.

Season

This identifies the season(s) you are most likely to find a bird within its range. Some birds are resident, meaning that they remain in one location throughout the year. Others may spend summers in one area and winters in another, briefly visiting the areas in between during spring and fall. Keep in mind there is always the possibility of a migrating bird remaining in an area longer than usual, or arriving earlier than usual, making the use of season only a general guide to identification.

Illustrations

Illustrations show the adult bird perched and in flight. If males and females differ considerably, I have included both sexes. Other plumages, such as those of juveniles and alternate morphs, are described in the text.

Bird Topography and Terms

Bird topography describes the outer surface of a bird and how its various anatomical structures fit together. Below are diagrams outlining the terms most commonly used to describe the feathers and bare parts of a bird: one of a diurnal raptor and one of an owl.

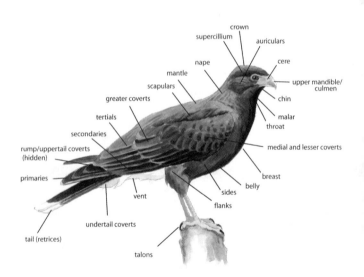

crown
supercillium
auriculars
nape
cere
mantle
upper mandible/culmen
scapulars
chin
greater coverts
malar
tertials
throat
secondaries
rump/uppertail coverts (hidden)
medial and lesser coverts
primaries
breast
vent
belly
sides
flanks
tail (retrices)
undertail coverts
talons

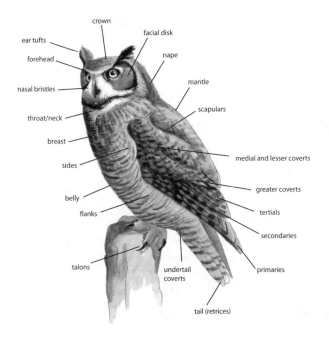

crown

facial disk

ear tufts

nape

forehead

mantle

nasal bristles

scapulars

throat/neck

breast

medial and lesser coverts

sides

greater coverts

belly

tertials

flanks

secondaries

talons

primaries

undertail
coverts

tail (retrices)

NEW WORLD VULTURES

California Condor, *Gymnogyps californianus*
Family Cathartidae (New World Vultures)
Size: 46"
Range: Isolated areas in southern California and northern Utah
Habitat: Mountains, canyons, open areas
Season: Year-round

The California Condor was saved from the brink of extinction by extensive human efforts and has been re-introduced in the South-west, but still leads a precarious existence in the wild. It is unmistakable because of its huge size (the wingspan reaches nine feet), noticeably larger than the eagles and other vultures. It is stocky with a rounded, featherless head that is grayish in juveniles and pink or reddish in adults. A distinct ruff of feathers encircles the neck. The plumage color is jet black except for white under-wing

linings and thin white edges to the upper wing coverts. In soaring flight, the wings are very broad, held level or slightly bent up, with well-slotted primaries. The tail is relatively short. They use their keen sense of sight to detect mammalian carcasses upon which to feed. The illustrations show an adult perched and in flight.

Black Vulture, *Coragyps atratus*
Family Cathartidae (New World Vultures)
Size: 25"
Range: Southeastern US; also in southern Arizona
Habitat: Open, dry country
Season: Year-round

Like the Turkey Vulture, the Black Vulture is adept at soaring. Its wing beats, however, are faster, and while soaring, it holds its wings at a flat angle instead of a dihedral, or upright V shape. It is stocky in physique, has a short, stubby tail, and shorter and broader wings than the Turkey Vulture. The primaries are pale on an otherwise black body, and the head is bald and gray. It eats carrion and garbage and is quite aggressive at feeding sites. The adult, perched and flying, is illustrated.

The Black Vulture is one of the few species that has actually benefited from deforestation. As forests in central and southern America have been cleared, more open space for vultures to soar and feed is available—leading populations to increase.

Turkey Vulture, *Cathartes aura*
Family Cathartidae (New World Vultures)
Size: 27"
Range: Throughout the US
Habitat: Open, dry country
Season: Summer in the interior and northern latitudes; year-round in lower latitudes and along the coasts

The Turkey Vulture is known for its effortless, skilled soaring. It will often soar for hours, without flapping, rocking in the breeze on 6-foot wings that form an upright V shape, or dihedral angle. It has a black body and inner wing, with pale flight feathers and pale tail feathers that give it a noticeable two-toned appearance from below. The tail is longish, and the feet extend no more than halfway past the base of the tail. The head is naked, red, and small, so the bird appears almost headless in flight. The bill is strongly hooked to aid in tearing apart its favored food—carrion. Juveniles have a dark gray head. Turkey Vultures often roost in flocks and form groups around food or at a roadkill site. The adult, perched and flying, is illustrated.

Unlike most birds, Turkey Vultures have a highly developed sense of smell, which helps them locate rotting carcasses from high in the air. Because Black Vultures lack this keen smelling ability, they will often tag along with Turkey Vultures to find food.

OSPREY

Osprey, *Pandion haliaetus*
Family Pandionidae (Osprey)
Size: 23"; female larger than male
Range: Summer; spring and fall migrant
Habitat: Always near water, salt or fresh
Season: Summer in northern latitudes; winter and year-round in lower latitudes

Also known as the Fish Hawk, the Osprey exhibits a dramatic feeding method: It plunges feet first into the water to snag fish. Sometimes it completely submerges itself, then laboriously flies off with its heavy catch. It is dark brown above and white below, and has a distinct dark eye stripe contiguous with the nape. Females

show a dark, mottled "necklace" across their breasts, and juveniles have pale streaking on their backs. Ospreys fly with an obvious crook at the wrist, appearing gull-like. Wings are long and narrow, with white under-wing linings and a dark carpal patch. The adult, perched and flying, is illustrated.

Hook-billed Kite, *Chondrohierax uncinatus*
Family Accipitridae (Raptors)
Size: 17"
Range: Central America into the southern tip of Texas
Habitat: Dense, leafy vegetation in trees, especially mesquite near water
Season: Year-round

The Hook-billed Kite is a small- to medium-size raptor found in the US only along the Rio Grande in southern Texas. The head is relatively large with a long, strongly hooked bill; the tail is long, and the wings are short, rounded, very broad, and noticeably constricted at the base. Both sexes have white eyes, wide tail bands, and barring on the wings and underparts. Males are slate

gray overall, while females are reddish orange below and dark brown above. Juveniles are similar to females but are whitish on the underparts and on the face. Hook-billed Kites typically clamber through vegetation, but in flight have floppy wing beats with wings held forward. Their favored prey is snails that live in trees. They clutch the snails with their talons and pry out the meat with their specialized bill; they will also eat small vertebrates. The illustrations show an adult perched and in flight.

13

Swallow-tailed Kite, *Elanoides forficatus*
Family Accipitridae (Raptors)
Size: 23"
Range: Far southeastern US
Habitat: Wooded environments, wetlands
Season: Summer

The Swallow-tailed Kite is a graceful, skilled flier that feeds on the wing, catching insects mid-air or snatching reptiles from tree branches. It even drinks by skimming along the water surface. It resembles a large swallow with its long, deeply forked tail and

long, thin wings. The body and head are white, and the back, tail, and wings are black. The bill is small and hooked, and the eye is dark. In flight from below, the white color of the body and wing linings contrast strongly with the black tail and flight feathers. Swallow-tailed Kites may flock together while feeding or during migration to and from their winter home in South America. The illustration shows an adult, perched and in flight.

HAWKS AND
EAGLES

White-tailed Kite, *Elanus leucurus*
Family Accipitridae (Hawks, Eagles)
Size: 15"
Range: West Coast, Florida, Texas
Habitat: Open grasslands with trees or thickets, roadsides
Season: Year-round
The White-tailed Kite, also known as the Black-shouldered Kite, is an elegant kite with long, pointed wings, a long tail, and a small, hooked bill. It is gray above, with a large black shoulder patch and a white tail. The underside and head are white, with gray on the

nape and black around the red eyes, giving an angry expression. Juveniles have brown streaking across the neck and on the crown. White-tailed Kites fly with a slight dihedral angle to the wings, and they have a black spots at the wrists on the otherwise pale under-wing. They patrol grasslands in the air or from a perch, and often hover before attacking their prey of rodents and reptiles. The adult, perched and in flight, is illustrated.

Snail Kite, *Rostrhamus sociabilis*
Family Accipitridae (Hawks and Eagles)
Size: 17"
Range: South-central Florida
Habitat: Freshwater marshes
Season: Year-round

Also known as the Everglade Kite, the Snail Kite is a tropical species with very specific feeding habits. It relies almost exclusively on a certain apple snail that it snatches from the grass while in flight. It then removes the flesh from the shell with its sharply hooked bill and sharp talons. The plumage is dark overall except for the front half of the tail, which is white. Males are dark slate gray with red

legs. Females are dark brown with a streaked breast and lighter facial markings. In flight, the Snail Kite displays a mostly dark body and wings with a white inner tail area, and in females, a pale base to the primaries from below. Florida is the only US state in which to find the Snail Kite, and its numbers are very sensitive to habitat changes and the availability of snails. The illustration shows a male (below) and a female (above), and the female in flight.

Mississippi Kite, *Ictinia mississippiensis*
Family Accipitridae (Kites, Hawks, Eagles)
Size: 14"
Range: Southeastern Colorado to the southeastern US
Habitat: Swamps, woodland edges, agricultural land
Season: Summer

The Mississippi Kite is North America's smallest kite, with a rounded head, short, hooked bill, and long wings and tail. Its plumage is slate gray across the back, undersides, and upper wing, with a paler head, becoming almost white. The tail and ends of the primaries are black, contrasting with the white secondaries. The lores and feathers surrounding the deep red eyes are black.

Sexes are similar, while juveniles show white spotting on the back and rufous spotting on the underside. In flight, wings are held flat and straight, and the outermost primary is noticeably shorter than the others. Mississippi Kites feed in flight, snatching insects from the air or swooping low to attack small terrestrial animals. The voice is a high-pitched, relatively weak whistle in two parts. The adult, perched and in flight, is illustrated.

Northern Harrier, *Circus cyaneus*
Family Accipitridae (Hawks, Eagles)
Size: 18"; female larger than male
Range: Throughout North America
Habitat: Open fields, wetlands
Season: Summer in northern latitudes, year-round in middle latitudes, and winter in southern latitudes of North America

Also known as the Marsh Hawk, the Northern Harrier flies low to the ground, methodically surveying its hunting grounds for rodents and other small animals. When it spots prey, aided by its acute hearing, it will drop abruptly to the ground to attack. It is a

thin raptor with a long tail and long, flame-shaped wings that are broad in the middle. The face has a distinct owl-like facial disk, and there is a conspicuous white patch at the rump. Males are gray above, with a white, streaked breast and black wingtips. Females are brown with a barred breast. The juvenile is similar in plumage to the female, but with a pale belly. The female (below) and male (above) are illustrated, in addition to a male in flight.

Bald Eagle, *Haliaeetus leucocephalus*
Family Accipitridae (Hawks, Eagles)
Size: 30–40"; female larger than male
Range: Throughout North America
Habitat: Lakes, rivers with tall perches or cliffs
Season: Summer in far northern latitudes; winter and year-round throughout most of the US

The Bald Eagle is a large raptor that is fairly uncommon even though its range is widespread. It eats fish or scavenges dead animals, and congregates in large numbers where food is abundant. Plumage is dark brown, which contrasts with its white head and tail. Juveniles show white splotching across the wings and breast. The yellow bill is large and powerful, and the talons are large and sharp. In flight the Bald Eagle holds its wings fairly flat and straight, resembling a long plank. Bald Eagles make huge nests of sticks high in trees. The adult, perched and flying, is illustrated.

Golden Eagle, *Aquila chrysaetos*
Family Accipitridae (Hawks, Eagles)
Size: 30"; female larger than male
Range: Throughout North America
Habitat: Mountainous areas, hills, open country
Season: Summer in far northern latitudes; year-round and winter in the continental US, especially in the western states

The Golden Eagle is a solitary, very large, buteo-shaped raptor with large talons and long, broad wings, with a 6.5-foot wingspan. Its plumage is dark brown overall, with a pale golden nape and a relatively small head. The bill is large and hooked, and forms a wide gape. The juvenile shows a white patch at the base of the tail and at the base of the flight feathers. Golden Eagles hold their wings horizontal or with a very slight dihedral angle in flight. They

forage from a perch or by soaring overhead, attacking mammals, reptiles, and birds. They may also eat carrion. The adult, perched and in flight, is illustrated.

Northern Goshawk, *Accipiter gentilis*
Family Accipitridae (Hawks, Eagles)
Size: 22"; female larger than male
Range: Northern latitudes of North America from Alaska to the southern Rocky Mountains
Habitat: Mountains, forests
Season: Year-round
The Northern Goshawk is North America's largest accipiter, similar in shape to the Cooper's and Sharp-shinned Hawks, but often mistaken for a buteo because of its large size. It is dark gray on the back and finely barred white and gray underneath. The head has a white superciliary stripe bordered by a dark crown and ear patch. Juveniles are mottled brown with coarse streaking across

the breast, and have more noticeably banded tails. Northern Goshawks hunt from a perch, ambush-style, flying through woodlands to capture birds and mammals up to rabbit size. The adult, perched and in flight, is illustrated.

Sharp-shinned Hawk, *Accipiter striatus*
Family Accipitridae (Hawks, Eagles)
Size: 10–14"; female larger than male
Range: Throughout North America
Habitat: Woodlands, bushy areas
Season: Summer in far northern latitudes; winter and year-round in most of the continental US

The Sharp-shinned Hawk is North America's smallest accipiter, with a longish, squared tail and stubby, rounded wings. Its short wings allow for agile flight in tight, wooded quarters, where it quickly attacks small birds in flight. It is grayish above and light below, barred with pale rufous stripes. The eyes are set forward on

the face to aid in the direct pursuit of prey. The juvenile is white below, streaked with brown. The Sharp-shinned Hawk may be confused with the larger Cooper's Hawk. The adult, perched and in flight, is illustrated.

Cooper's Hawk, *Accipiter cooperii*
Family Accipitridae (Hawks, Eagles)
Size: 17"; female larger than male
Range: Throughout the continental US
Habitat: Woodlands
Season: Year-round

The Cooper's Hawk perches stealthily on branches in the canopy, then ambushes its prey of smaller birds or mammals by diving through thickets. Its plumage is very similar to that of the Sharp-shinned Hawk, although it is larger in size, has a slightly longer, rounded tail and thinner wings, and sports a relatively larger head. The eyes are set in the middle of the face. Unlike Sharp-shinned Hawks, Cooper's Hawks may perch and hunt in open country. The adult, perched and in flight, is illustrated.

Both Cooper's and Sharp-shinned Hawks are adapted to flying fast and making quick turns around trees, thickets, fences, or other backyard obstructions. This ability, combined with the element of surprise, makes them a constant threat to songbirds trying to enjoy a meal at your birdfeeder—especially if it's in an exposed location.

Common Black-hawk, *Buteogallus anthracinus*
Family Accipitridae (Hawks, Eagles)
Size: 21"
Range: Southwestern US: Arizona, New Mexico and Texas into Mexico and Central America
Habitat: Wooded areas near water
Season: Summer in the US

The Common Black-hawk is a robust, large, dark hawk that thrives in the arid Southwest along permanent streams with wooded banks. The secondaries and tertials are very long, forming broad, deep wings when outstretched, and the tail is very short and broad. The adult is completely black except for a wide, white tail band, a thin, white terminal tail band, and pale, silvery bases on the

underside of all flight feathers. The pale bill appears large because of the yellow cere and extensive facial skin, and the longish legs are bright yellow. Juveniles have several thin tail bands, streaked underparts, and whitish speckles on the outer wing. Common Black-hawks hunt for small reptiles, amphibians, and fish that haunt the riparian zone, often from a perch just above the water. Flapping flight is slow and methodical, and gliding is on relatively flat wings. The voice consists of rapidly repeated, ascending, shrill *kwee* notes. The adult, flying and perched, is illustrated.

Harris's Hawk, *Parabuteo unicinctus*
Family Accipitridae (Hawks, Eagles)
Size: 20"; female larger than male
Range: Southwestern US
Habitat: Arid open woodlands, scrub, desert
Season: Year-round

The Harris's Hawk is a somewhat lanky buteo with a long tail and legs and a smallish head. It is dark brown overall with chestnut shoulders, under-wing coverts, and thighs. The base of the tail is white above and below, and there is a white terminal band, forming a broad black band across the tail. Juveniles show pale streaking on the breast. Harris's Hawks hunt by coursing low over the ground, searching for mammals to rabbit size, reptiles, and insects. They perch on poles and tall cacti, often in a horizontal

posture. Their range extends into South America, where they are known as Bay-winged Hawks because of their broad, paddlelike wings. The adult, perched and in flight, is illustrated.

Gray Hawk, *Buteo nitidus*
Family Accipitridae (Hawks, Eagles)
Size: 17"
Range: Far southern Arizona and Texas, into Mexico
Habitat: Wooded areas near water, especially near cottonwoods, willow, and mesquite
Season: Summer in southern Arizona, year-round in southern Texas
The Gray Hawk is a small buteo with an extensive range in South and Central America but reaching only just above the Mexican border in the US. It is handsomely patterned with a slate-gray back and head, finely barred white and gray underside, dark eyes and bill, and a yellow cere and legs. The tail is relatively long with contrasting black and white bands. In flight, the wings are broad

and rounded with dark tips to the flight feathers and a very pale underside. Juveniles are brown above and white below with chunky brown spots and streaks. Gray Hawks hunt from perches in trees or by flying along woodland edges in search of lizards on the ground. Their flight style resembles an accipiter, with quick flapping mixed with short glides. The voice is a two-part, high-pitched, ascending *who-eee,* or a longer, shrill, descending one-note call. The adult, perched and flying, is illustrated.

Red-shouldered Hawk, *Buteo lineatus*
Family Accipitridae (Hawks, Eagles)
Size: 17"
Range: Eastern US; also California
Habitat: Wooded areas near water
Season: Year-round

The Red-shouldered Hawk is a solitary, small, accipiter-like buteo with a long tail. It waits patiently on its perch before flying down to attack a variety of small animals. It has a banded black-and-white tail and spotted dark wings. The head and shoulder are rust-colored, while the breast is light with rust barring. The legs are

long and yellow, and the bill is hooked. In flight, there is a pale arc just inside the wingtips, and it flaps its wings with quick beats followed by short glides. Western populations are darker overall than their eastern counterparts. The adult, perched and flying, is illustrated.

Broad-winged Hawk, *Buteo platypterus*
Family Accipitridae (Hawks, Eagles)
Size: 15"
Range: Eastern North America
Habitat: Woodlands, roadsides
Season: Summer

The Broad-winged Hawk is North America's smallest buteo. It summers in southern Canada and the eastern US and migrates in huge flocks to Central and South America in the winter. It is dark brown above, white below, with a reddish-brown breast that fades to spotting and barring across the belly and flanks. A rare dark morph is dark brown overall. Both morphs have wide black-and-white bars across the tail; less developed in juvenile birds. In flight, there is a dark border to the trailing edge of the other-wise light under-wing, and the wings are held flat while soaring.

Broad-winged Hawks hunt for small mammals, reptiles, amphibians, or invertebrates, often near a water source. Their voice is a piercing, very high-pitched *pe-seeee*. The adult light morph, perched and in flight, is illustrated.

Short-tailed Hawk, *Buteo brachyurus*
Family Accipitridae (Hawks and Eagles)
Size: 16"
Range: Florida; rare in southern Arizona
Habitat: Forest or mixed woodland/grassland
Season: Year-round in southern Florida; vagrant to southern Arizona

The reclusive Short-tailed Hawk is a smallish, plump buteo with rounded wings and a short tail. The slim forehead runs contiguous with the upper bill, giving a flat-headed appearance. Two color morphs exist: The dark morph, more common in Florida, is dark brown overall with light wing linings, and the light morph has clean white underparts. In flight, it holds its wings flat with the tips bending up. To feed, it kites above the treetops and plunges

to capture prey. Florida is the only state in which to find this tropical species in the US, except for rare sightings in southern Arizona. The illustration shows an adult dark morph, perched and in flight.

Swainson's Hawk, *Buteo swainsoni*
Family Accipitridae (Hawks, Eagles)
Size: 19"; female larger than male
Range: Western half of North America, except for coastal areas
Habitat: Dry prairies, open fields
Season: Summer

The Swainson's Hawk is a buteo with a long tail, long wings with pointed tips, and a relatively small, rounded head. It has variable plumage colors, ranging from dark morphs to the more common light morphs. The light morph has a white underside, a dark brown back, a rufous breast, and white lores and chin. Darker forms become rufous or dark brown on the breast and belly. In flight the light morph has pale wing linings and a pale belly that contrasts with its darker flight feathers and tail. Swainson's Hawks feed on small mammals, insects, and reptiles, either descending

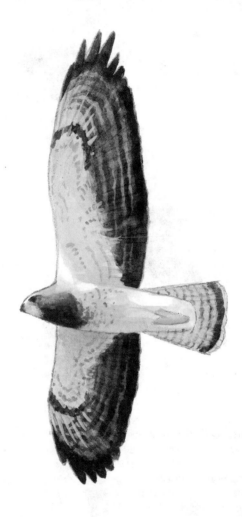

from a perch or by stalking on the ground. The hawk's voice is a high-pitched *eeeeww*. The light morph adult is illustrated, perched and in flight.

White-tailed Hawk, *Buteo albicaudatus*
Family Accipitridae (Hawks, Eagles)
Size: 20–23"; female larger than male
Range: Southeastern Texas
Habitat: Coastal plains, grasslands
Season: Year-round
A Texas specialty, the White-tailed Hawk is a stocky buteo with long, narrow wings and a short, white tail with a black subterminal band. The head and back are slate gray, the wings are dark

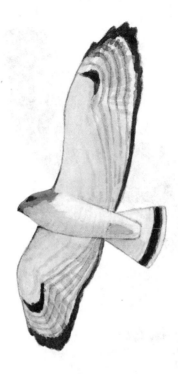

gray, and the shoulder region is rust-colored. The throat and underparts are white in the adult, but juvenile birds show dark barring on the belly and have a dark throat. From a perch or from flight, White-tailed Hawks capture insects and small vertebrates in the grass or scrub. They may also hunt at the edges of grassland fires where prey is scattering from the flames.

Zone-tailed Hawk, *Buteo albonotatus*
Family Accipitridae (Hawks, Eagles)
Size: 20"
Range: Southwestern US into Central America
Habitat: Open woodlands, scrub, often near canyons and streams
Season: Summer

The Zone-tailed Hawk is a large, dark buteo that, while soaring, can be mistaken for a Turkey Vulture. They often perch upright on tree branches, showing a stocky posture with short, yellow legs, a short, pale bill, and a long tail and wingtips. Both sexes are uniformly dark gray to black, with a paler, finely barred interior of the underside of the flight feathers (even lighter in juveniles). The tail has two or three light bars, gray from above and white from below, with the outermost bar being the most prominent. In soaring flight, the wings are quite long and narrow, being of

nearly equal width throughout their length, and the tail is long and narrow. Zone-tailed Hawks hold their wings in a prominent dihedral and tilt side to side, much like Turkey Vultures. They hunt small vertebrates or reptiles by stooping from high in the air or from low, patrolling flight. The voice is a harsh, penetrating *keer*, similar to that of a Red-tailed Hawk.

Red-tailed Hawk, *Buteo jamaicensis*
Family Accipitridae (Hawks, Eagles)
Size: 20"
Range: Throughout North America
Habitat: Prairies, open country
Season: Year-round

This widespread species is the most common buteo in the US. It has broad, rounded wings and a stout, hooked bill. Its plumage is highly variable depending on geographic location. In general the underparts are light, with darker streaking that forms a dark band across the belly, the upperparts are dark brown, and the tail is rufous. Light spotting occurs along the scapulars. In flight there is a noticeable dark patch along the inner leading edge of the under wing. Red-tailed Hawks glide down from perches, such

as telephone poles and posts in open country, to catch rodents. They also may hover to spot prey. They are usually seen alone or in pairs. The voice is the familiar *keeer!* The western adult, perched and in flight, is illustrated.

Ferruginous Hawk, *Buteo regalis*
Family Accipitridae (Hawks, Eagles)
Size: 23"; female larger than male
Range: Western half of the US
Habitat: Dry prairies, open country
Season: Year-round
The Ferruginous Hawk is North America's largest buteo. It has a thick body and neck, a large, hooked bill, and long, broad wings. Two color morphs occur: light and dark. The light morph is white below with rufous barring on the flanks and thighs. The back is mottled brown and rufous, with grayish flight feathers. The dark morph is dark brown overall, with white on the undersides of the flight feathers and tail. Ferruginous Hawks stalk their prey of small mammals from a perch, or by hovering or soaring. The light morph adult, perched and in flight, is illustrated.

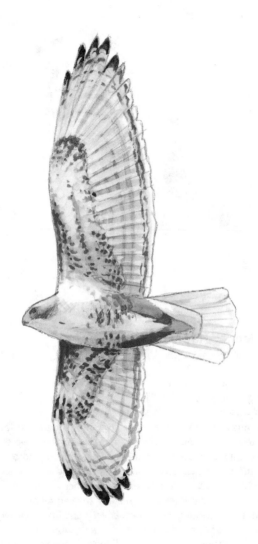

Rough-legged Hawk, *Buteo lagopus*
Family Accipitridae (Hawks, Eagles)
Size: 21"
Range: Throughout North America
Habitat: Open country, areas near cliffs
Season: Winter in the contiguous US, summer in Alaska

The Rough-legged Hawk is a relatively long-winged and long-tailed buteo with a proportionately small bill and feet. Two color phases exist, light and dark, with the light phase being most common. It is mottled dark brown or grayish above, and mixed creamy white and dark brown below, often with a concentration of dark at the belly, especially in females. In flight, the central part of the wing is white, contrasting with darker coverts and tips of the flight feathers. The tail has a white base and a dark subterminal band. The legs are feathered for arctic conditions (hence the common

name). Rough-legged Hawks search for small mammals or ground birds from a perch or while in flight, often hovering overhead. The light-phase adult, perched and in flight, is illustrated.

FALCONS

Crested Caracara, *Caracara cheriway*
Family Falconidae (Falcons)
Size: 23"
Range: Southern Arizona, eastern Texas, central Florida
Habitat: Dry prairies and scrubland
Season: Year-round

The Crested Caracara is a falcon that is somewhat vulture-like in its behavior. It forages on carcasses or immobile prey, which it finds by soaring on flat wings or cruising over pastures and open savanna. It may also perch on poles or on the ground. Its head seems large for its body and it has a long neck and long legs. It is an overall dark bird with a white neck, black cap, and large, hooked bill. The face has a large patch of reddish bare skin. In

flight the white wingtips and tail are distinctive. This tropical falcon is rare in the US and was once a threatened species here. The illustration shows an adult, perched and in flight.

American Kestrel, *Falco sparverius*
Family Falconidae (Falcons)
Size: 10"
Range: Throughout North America
Habitat: Open country, urban areas
Season: Year-round

North America's most common falcon, the American Kestrel is a tiny, robin-size falcon with long, pointed wings and tail, and fast flight. It hovers above fields or dives from a perch in branches or on a wire to capture small animals and insects. The kestrel's upperparts are rufous and barred with black, its wings are blue-gray, and its breast is buff colored or white and streaked with black spots. The head is patterned with a gray crown and vertical patches of black down the face. The female has rufous wings

and a barred tail. Also known as the Sparrow Hawk, the kestrel has a habit of flicking its tail up and down while perched. The adult male is illustrated.

Merlin, *Falco columbarius*
Family Falconidae (Falcons)
Size: 10–12"; female larger than males
Range: Throughout North America
Habitat: Open country, woodland edges, farmland
Season: Winter in the contiguous US, summer in Canada and Alaska

The Merlin is a pugnacious, stocky falcon, slightly larger and heavier than a Kestrel, with pointed wings and a short, stubby bill. Three subspecies are recognized, with varying degrees of darkness in plumage. In general, the upperparts are some shade of gray (in males) or brown (in females), with variable amounts of light to dark brown streaking. Light individuals have only a faint

moustacial patch, while dark individuals may have a mostly dark head. In flight, notice the dark tail with thin, pale bands. Merlins pursue small birds in direct, powerful flight, or in sudden stoops. The adult male, perched and in flight, is illustrated.

Gyrfalcon, *Falco rusticolus*
Family Falconidae (Falcons)
Size: 22"; female larger than male
Range: Northern latitudes of the US, into Canada and Alaska
Habitat: Open country near cliffs
Season: Winter in the contiguous US, year-round in Alaska

The Gyrfalcon is a large, powerful falcon of the north with a long tail and somewhat more rounded wings than other falcons. Three color morphs exist: white, gray, and dark. The gray form is slate-gray above, heavily barred with white and gray below, and has dark facial markings across the eye and malar area. The white morph is snow-white with dark gray mottling on the back, tail,

and wings. The dark morph is grayish brown overall with white mottling on the breast, a pale chin, and pale grayish flight feathers when seen from below. Gyrfalcons pursue birds and mammals up to duck and rabbit size in direct flight on stiff wings. The adult gray phase, perched and flying, is illustrated.

Peregrine Falcon, *Falco peregrinus*
Family Falconidae (Falcons)
Size: 17"; female larger than male
Range: Throughout North America
Habitat: Open country, cliffs, urban areas
Season: All seasons

The Peregrine Falcon is a powerful and agile raptor with long, sharply pointed wings. It is dark, slate gray above and pale whitish below, with uniform barring below the breast. Plumage on the head forms a distinctive "helmet," with a white ear patch and chin contrasting with the blackish face and crown. Juveniles are mottled brown overall, with heavy streaking on the underside. Peregrine Falcons attack other birds in flight using spectacular high-speed aerial dives. Once threatened by DDT pollution that

caused thinning of their eggshells, the Peregrine Falcon has made a dramatic comeback. The adult, perched and in flight, is illustrated.

Prairie Falcon, *Falco mexicanus*
Family Falconidae (Falcons)
Size: 17"; female larger than male
Range: Eastern half of the US
Habitat: Prairies, open land near cliffs and mountains
Season: Year-round

The Prairie Falcon is large, with a long tail and narrow, pointed wings. The body is pale brown-gray above, and white below with brown streaking. The head is patterned with a white ear patch and chin, a dark malar patch, and a large, black eye. The underside in flight is marked with dark inner-wing coverts and axillar (armpit) feathers. Prairie Falcons attack small animals on the ground from a perch or after aerial pursuit. The adult, perched and in flight, is illustrated.

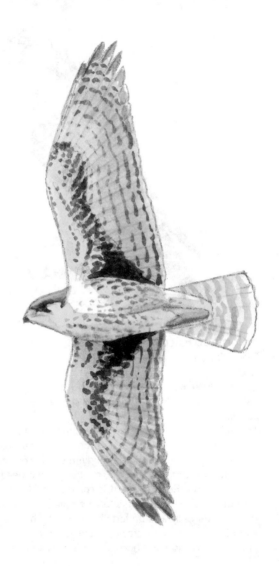

Aplomado Falcon, *Falco femoralis*
Family Falconidae (Falcons)
Size: 16"
Range: Very rare in sections of southeastern Texas
Habitat: Arid, open grasslands with cactus and yucca
Season: Year-round

The Aplomado Falcon was mostly extirpated from the US in the early 1900s but is now being reintroduced in southeastern Texas from captive-bred birds. It is a medium-size falcon, slight in stature, with a very long, thin tail, relatively large head, and long, thin, pointed wings. The adult is colorful and vividly patterned, with mostly dark wings, white breast, dark brown belly, and pale rufous lower belly and undertail coverts. The head is white with a bold black eye stripe, crown, forehead, and bar below the eye, and the bill is short and hooked. In flight, from above, it appears

uniformly dark gray with thin, pale barring on the tail. Juveniles are buff rather than white on the head and breast, and the breast is streaked with dark brown. Aplomado Falcons hunt large insects, small birds or reptiles, mostly during twilight hours, snatching prey by stooping from a perch or by direct, chasing flight. The voice is a series of shrill *keek-keek-keek* notes.

SHRIKES

Loggerhead Shrike, *Lanius ludovicianus*
Family Laniidae (Shrikes)
Size: 9.5"
Range: Throughout the contiguous US
Habitat: Dry open country
Season: Year-round; summer only in northern latitudes

The solitary Loggerhead Shrike is not technically a bird of prey, but it is mentioned here because of its raptorlike feeding habits. It swoops down from its perch on a branch, wire, or post and captures large insects, small mammals, or birds, impaling them on thorny barbs before tearing them apart to feed. Similar to the Northern Shrike, which is a winter resident, it has a compact, large head and a short, thick, slightly hooked bill. The upperparts are gray, and the underparts are pale. The wings are black, with white patches at the base of the primaries and upper coverts. The tail is black and edged with white. There is a black mask on the head extending from the base of the bill to the ear area. Juveniles show a finely barred breast. It flies with quick wing beats and swooping glides. The adult, perched and in flight, is illustrated.

The shrike's gruesome habit of impaling prey on thorns or barbed wire, or forcing it into a tight crevice, secures the prey so the shrike can feed efficiently. The true raptors have strong talons (compared to the relatively weak ones of the shrikes) that hold their prey secure.

Northern Shrike, *Lanius excubitor*
Family Laniidae (Shrikes)
Size: 10"
Range: Northern latitudes of the US, into Canada and Alaska
Habitat: Dry open country
Season: Winter in the contiguous US, summer in Alaska

The Northern Shrike is similar to the slightly smaller Loggerhead Shrike and shares its raptorial feeding habits. It has a large head and a medium-length, thick, moderately hooked bill. The upperparts are light gray with a white rump, and the underparts are pale and finely barred. The wings are black, with white patches at the base of the primaries and upper coverts. The tail is black and edged with white. There is a black mask on the head extending from the base of the bill to the ear area, but this does not extend above the eye. It flies with quick wing beats and swooping glides. The adult, perched and in flight, is illustrated.

BARN OWL

Barn Owl, *Tyto alba*
Family Tytonidae (Barn Owl)
Size: 23"
Range: Throughout the US except for the north-central region
Habitat: Barns, farmland, open areas with mature trees
Season: Year-round
The Barn Owl is a large-headed pale owl with small dark eyes, a
heart-shaped facial disk, and long feathered legs. The wings, back,
tail, and crown are light rusty brown with light gray smudging and
small white dots. The underside, face, and under-wing linings are
white, with spots of rust on the breast. Females are usually darker
than males, with more color and spotting across the breast and
sides. The facial disk is enclosed by a thin line of dark feathers. In

flight from below it is nearly all white with faint barring on the flight feathers. Barn Owls are nocturnal hunters for rodents, and their call is a haunting, raspy *screeee!* The adult male, perched and in flight, is illustrated.

TYPICAL OWLS

Flammulated Owl, *Otus flammeolus*
Family Strigidae (Typical Owls)
Size: 6.75"
Range: Western US
Habitat: Mid- to higher elevation dry, coniferous, or mixed woodlands
Season: Summer

The Flammulated Owl is a small, dark-eyed, large-headed, nocturnal owl, closely related to the Screech Owl, with short ear tufts that are normally pressed into the head. Plumage is cryptically mottled in grays, white, black, and rufous (*flammulated* means "reddish"). Southern birds are more rufous, while northern birds are grayer overall. A paler edge to the scapulars may form a

distinct V shape across the back. In flight from below, the plumage is rather dark and heavily mottle, and the wings are relatively
long and rounded. Flammulated Owls feed at night on insects,
including moths and beetles, in foliage, on the ground, or in
flight. Their voice consists of low hoots, either singly or in a series
of two short and one longer hoot. They nest in tree cavities and
migrate south for the winter. The adult, perched and in flight, is
illustrated.

Whiskered Screech Owl, *Megascops trichopsis*
Family Strigidae (Typical Owls)
Size: 7"
Range: Southeastern Arizona
Habitat: High-elevation forested mountains and canyons, especially among oaks
Season: Year-round

This elusive owl is mostly found in Mexico and Central America but ranges into the US in southern Arizona. It stays high in the tree canopy and is most active at night, making it difficult to see, but can be readily identified by its unique voice: a somewhat irregular series of soft toots, varying between staccato notes, pauses, and longer notes. It is often likened to a Morse code type of pattern.

The Whiskered Screech Owl appears like small version of the Western Screech Owl with large, golden-yellow eyes, a black-bordered facial disk, prominent ear tufts (may be pressed into the head), and overall grayish color. The breast is heavily barred with black, and long whiskers appear at either side of the bill. In flight, wings are short, broad, and rounded, and show dark carpal patches on the underside. These owls hunt in foliage or in mid-air for flying insects, beetles, grasshoppers, or small mammals. The adult, perched and in flight, is illustrated.

Western Screech Owl, *Megascops kennicottii*
Family Strigidae (Typical Owls)
Size: 8.5"
Range: Western US
Habitat: Wooded areas or parks; places where cavity-bearing trees exist
Season: Year-round

The Western Screech Owl is a small, eared owl with a big head, short tail, and bright yellow eyes. The highly camouflaged plumage ranges from brown to gray, depending on the region. It is darker above, streaked and barred below. The ear tufts may be

drawn back to give the appearance of a rounded head, and the bill is grayish green tipped with white. White spots on the margins of the coverts and scapulars create two white bars on the folded wing. It is a nocturnal bird, hunting during the night for small mammals, insects, or fish. Its voice is a series of hoots that gradually speed up in tempo. It can appear very similar to the Eastern Screech Owl, but their ranges do not usually overlap. The adult, perched and in flight, is illustrated.

Eastern Screech Owl, *Megascops asio*
Family Strigidae (Typical Owls)
Size: 8.5"
Range: Central and eastern US
Habitat: Wooded areas or parks, places where cavity-bearing trees exist
Season: Year-round

The Eastern Screech Owl is a small but big-headed, eared owl with a short tail and bright yellow eyes. Like that of the Western Screech Owl, the highly camouflaged plumage ranges from reddish to brown to gray, depending on region, but tends to be browner in the eastern part of its range. It is darker above, and streaked and barred below. The ear tufts may be drawn back

to give the appearance of a rounded head, and the bill is gray-ish green tipped with white. White spots on the margins of the coverts and scapulars create two white bars on the folded wing. It is a nocturnal bird, hunting during the night for small mammals, insects, or fish. Voice is a descending whistling call or a rapid stac-cato of one pitch. The adult, perched and in flight, is illustrated.

Great Horned Owl, *Bubo virginianus*
Family Strigidae (Typical Owls)
Size: 22"
Range: Throughout North America
Habitat: Almost any environment, from forests to plains to urban areas
Season: Year-round

Found throughout North America, the Great Horned Owl is a large, strong owl with an obvious facial disk and sharp, long tal-ons. Plumage is variable: Eastern forms are brown overall with

heavy barring, a rust-colored face, and a white chin patch, while western forms are grayer. The prominent ear tufts give the owl its name, and the eyes are large and yellow. The Great Horned Owl has exceptional hearing and sight. It feeds at night, perching on branches or posts, then swooping down on silent wings to catch birds, snakes, or mammals up to the size of a cat. Its voice is a low *hoo-hoo-hoo*. The adult, perched and in flight, is illustrated.

Snowy Owl, *Bubo scandiacus*
Family Strigidae (Typical Owls)
Size: 23"
Range: Northern latitudes of the US into Canada and Alaska
Habitat: Open grasslands
Season: Winter in the southern part of its range, year-round in the far north

The Snowy Owl is a large owl of the north with a smooth, domed head, feathered feet, and golden-yellow eyes. The plumage of the male is nearly pure white overall, only lightly spotted with black on the back and crown, and barred on the breast with gray. Females and juveniles have more extensive dark markings but

always show a white face. Snowy Owls are most active at twilight, swooping down to snatch small mammals or birds, favoring lemmings, especially on their breeding grounds. The adult male, perched and in flight, is illustrated.

Northern Hawk Owl, *Surnia ulula*
Family Strigidae (Typical Owls)
Size: 16"
Range: Northern latitudes of the US into Canada and Alaska
Habitat: Open woodlands, forest edges
Season: Winter at the southern edge of its range, year-round elsewhere
The Northern Hawk Owl is a fierce-looking owl of the northern forests with relatively pointed wings and a distinctive, long pointed tail. Adults are dark brown above with white spotting on the back and wings, and white below, with extensive, thin, brown barring. The facial disk is whitish and bordered on the sides with dark brown. The eyes and bill are yellow. In flight, the plumage

looks mottled dark overall except for the distinctive facial pat-
terning. Northern Hawk Owls are active primarily during the day,
feeding on small mammals and birds. The adult, perched and in
flight, is illustrated.

Northern Pygmy-Owl, *Glaucidium gnoma*
Family Strigidae (Typical Owls)
Size: 6.75"
Range: Western US
Habitat: Mixed woodlands, wooded riparian areas
Season: Year-round
The Northern Pygmy-Owl is a tiny but tough owl with a compact, round body, bright yellow eyes, and a long tail. The upperparts and head are brown with white spotting; the tail is brown with white bars. The underparts are white with broad, dark brown streaks, while the flanks, sides, and breast are brown (gray morphs

are also present, with grayish in place of the brown). White eyebrows continue to the bill, and the throat is white (not often visible on the perched bird). This fierce bird hunts mostly during twilight hours for insects or vertebrates, sometimes taking prey as big as itself. The voice is a short, soft, repeated *hoot* from high in the trees; the owl may be lured into view by imitating its call. Its flight is undulating on short, rounded wings. The adult, perched and in flight, is illustrated.

Ferruginous Pygmy-Owl, *Glaucidium brasilianum*
Family Strigidae (Typical Owls)
Size: 6.5"
Range: Far southwestern US
Habitat: Low-elevation deserts, arid riparian zones, areas with saguaro cactus or mesquite
Season: Year-round

The Ferruginous Pygmy-Owl is a tiny owl of Central America whose range comes into the US just in southern Arizona and the southernmost tip of Texas. It has a round, earless head, golden yellow eyes and feet, a fairly long, narrow tail, and short, rounded wings. The color is reddish-brown mottled with white above, and white

below with heavy brownish streaks and solid brown sides. The tail is barred in dark brown and paler reddish-brown. The forehead is specked with small white spots, and the hind neck is marked with black "eye spots." The similar Northern Pygmy-Owl has a range farther north, lives in higher elevations, and has whitish tail stripes and spotting rather than streaking on the forehead. Unlike most owls, Ferruginous Pygmy-Owls hunt during twilight hours or at daytime for a wide variety of insects and small vertebrates, either by hopping about through the vegetation or by quick, fast flight. They use nest holes found in trees or cacti. The voice is a quick, even-paced series of high, tooting or chirping notes like *poop-oop-oop-oop*. The adult, perched and in flight, is illustrated.

Elf Owl, *Micrathene whitneyi*
Family Strigidae (Typical Owls)
Size: 5.75"
Range: Far southwestern US near the Mexican border
Habitat: Desert with saguaro cactus; wooded streamsides
Season: Summer
The Elf Owl is a minute owl, the smallest in North America, that spends summer in the southwestern US and winter in Mexico. It has a proportionately small head that is narrower than the body, a short tail, bright yellow eyes, and no ear tufts. The overall color consists of pale earth tones: mottled gray, brown and buff on the

back and wings with large white spots at the base of the scapulars and mantle. The underside is whitish with variable reddish brown streaking. On the head is a distinct buff facial disk with white eyebrows that extend to the base of the bill. Flight is quick and direct with broad, rounded wings that are barred brownish and tawny with white spotting on the upper wing. Elf Owls feed on insects and other invertebrates such as scorpions and spiders. They build a nest in natural cavities or abandoned woodpecker holes in cacti or large trees. The voice is a series of yapping or mewing notes. The adult, perched and in flight, is illustrated.

Burrowing Owl, *Athene cunicularia*
Family Strigidae (Typical Owls)
Size: 9.5"
Range: Western half of the US
Habitat: Open grasslands and plains
Season: Summer in most of its range; year-round in California and southwestern states

The Burrowing Owl is a ground-dwelling owl that lives in burrows that rodents have vacated. It is small and flat-headed, and has a short tail and long legs. Plumage above is brown spotted with white, and extensively barred brown and white below. It

has a white chin and throat, and bright yellow eyes. Burrowing Owls can be seen day or night perched on the ground or on posts, scanning for insects and small rodents. Sometimes they exhibit a bowing movement when approached. The voice is a chattering or cooing, and sometimes imitative of a rattlesnake. The adult is illustrated.

Spotted Owl, *Strix occidentalis*
Family Strigidae (Typical Owls)
Size: 18"
Range: Pacific and southwestern states
Habitat: Old-growth woodlands
Season: Year-round

The Spotted Owl is a docile, medium-size, crestless owl with large black eyes and a short tail. The upperparts and head are dark brown with extensive white spotting, while the underside is whitish or light brown with dark brown barring (unlike the streaking of the similar Barred Owl). The bill is dull yellow, and the feet are mostly feathered. The voice is a throaty, booming, repeated

hoo-hoo-hoo or a high-pitched, ascending squeak. These owls are nocturnal, hunting through the night for small mammals. Spotted Owls have declined in numbers because of the destruction of old-growth forests, upon which they rely for nesting cavities. The adult, perched and in flight, is illustrated.

Barred Owl, *Strix varia*
Family Strigidae (Typical Owls)
Size: 21"
Range: Pacific Northwest and eastern US
Habitat: Wooded swamps, upland forests
Season: Year-round
The Barred Owl is a large owl with a short tail and wings, rounded head, and big, dark eyes. It lacks ear tufts and has comparatively small talons. Plumage is gray-brown overall with dark barring on the neck and breast, turning to streaking on the belly and flanks. It swoops from its perch to catch small rodents, frogs, or snakes.

Its voice, often heard during the day, is a hooting, *who-cooks-for-you,* or a kind of bark. Its nests are made in tree cavities vacated by other species. The illustration shows an adult, perched and in flight.

Great Gray Owl, *Strix nebulosa*
Family Strigidae (Typical Owls)
Size: 27"
Range: Northern parts of the Midwest and the Rocky Mountains, into Canada and Alaska
Habitat: Mixed and coniferous woodlands near clearings
Season: Year-round
The Great Gray Owl is the largest owl by length, although it is lighter than the Snowy Owl. It is large-headed and relatively long-tailed, with cryptically colored, thick plumage. It is mottled with light and dark shades of gray overall, except for a distinct

black-and-white, patterned chin patch, like a bow tie. The eyes are yellow and seem small compared to the head. Great Gray Owls are mostly nocturnal, but may also be active during the day in the summer season. They feed on small mammals and birds, and their voice consists of mid-range, repeated *woo-hoo* notes. The adult, perched and in flight, is illustrated.

Long-eared Owl, *Asio otus*
Family Strigidae (Typical Owls)
Size: 15"
Range: Throughout the contiguous US
Habitat: Dense woodlands near clearings or fields
Season: Summer in the northern latitudes, winter in the southern latitudes, year-round in between

The Long-eared Owl is a cryptic, nocturnal owl with a slender body, relatively long wings, and conspicuous ear tufts. The plumage is mottled gray-brown above, and pale with dark streaking below.

The bright yellow-orange eyes are in the middle of dark, vertical stripes, enclosed in a pale orange facial disk. They can compress their bodies vertically to appear as part of the tree branches. During the night, using their keen sense of hearing, Long-eared Owls fly on silent wings to hunt small rodents or birds. Their typical call is a series of low, well-spaced *hoo* notes. The adult is illustrated.

Short-eared Owl, *Asio flammeus*
Family Strigidae (Typical Owls)
Size: 15"
Range: Throughout North America
Habitat: Open country, marshes
Season: Summer in the northern latitudes, winter in the southern latitudes, year-round in between

Worldwide in distribution, the Short-eared Owl is a medium-size, large-headed owl with long wings and short, inconspicuous ear tufts. Plumage is mottled brown across the back and wings, and is whitish (in males) or buff (in females) underneath with brown

streaking down the breast. The facial disk is well formed, with bright yellow eyes surrounded by patches of black. When it is in flight, with slow and loping wing beats, note the large pale patch at the base of the primaries. Short-eared Owls are commonly active in twilight hours, and fly low over fields like a harrier, in search of small rodents. Its voice is a raspy, barking *chek-chek-chek*. The adult, perched and in flight, is illustrated.

Boreal Owl, *Aegolius funereus*
Family Strigidae (Typical Owls)
Size: 10"
Range: Northern latitudes of the US, including the Rocky Mountains, into Canada and Alaska
Habitat: Mixed forests
Season: Year-round
The Boreal Owl is a small owl of northern latitudes with a relatively large, flattish head and small, yellow eyes. The white facial disk is framed by black, and the forehead is black with extensive white dotting. The body is brownish with white spotting above,

and white below, streaked with brown. Active at dusk or night, the Boreal Owl attacks small mammals or insects by flying down from a perch, and voices a series of low-pitched, staccato toots, sometimes of extended duration. Their small size, nocturnal nature, and preference for wooded areas often make these owls difficult to spot. The adult, perched and in flight, is illustrated.

Northern Saw-whet Owl, *Aegolius acadicus*
Family Strigidae (Typical Owls)
Size: 8"
Range: Throughout the contiguous US into southern Alaska
Habitat: Coniferous or mixed woodlands
Season: Year-round
The Northern Saw-whet Owl is a very small, compact owl with a big head, large yellow-orange eyes, and a very short tail. Adults are brown above, with spotting along the scapulars and wing

coverts. Underparts are white, with thick brown streaking across the breast and sides. The facial disk lacks an obvious dark border, and the bill is black. Juveniles are blackish brown above, plain rufous below, with a distinct white patch on the forehead. Saw-whet Owls stay hidden in trees by day and forage during the night for small rodents. The voice is a repeating series of short, high *hoo* notes. The adult is illustrated.

Index

About the Author/Illustrator

Todd Telander is a naturalist, illustra-
tor, and artist living in Walla Walla,
Washington. He has studied and illustrated wildlife since 1989, while living
in California, Colorado, New Mexico,
and Washington state. He graduated
from the University of California at
Santa Cruz with degrees in biology,
environmental studies, and scientific
illustration, and has illustrated numer-
ous books and other publications,
including FalconGuides' Scats and Tracks series. He and his wife,
Kirsten Telander, a writer, run the Telander Gallery in downtown
Walla Walla. His work can be viewed online at toddtelander.com
or telandergallery.com.